RuPaul
In His Own Words

RuPaul
In His Own Words

EDITED BY
RACHEL HINTON
AND
HELENA HUNT

AN AGATE IMPRINT

CHICAGO

Printed in the United States

Library of Congress Cataloging-in-Publication Data

Names: RuPaul, 1960- author. | Hinton, Rachel, editor. | Hunt, Helena, editor.
Title: RuPaul in his own words / edited by Rachel Hinton and Helena Hunt.
Description: Chicago : B2 Books, an Agate imprint, [2020] | Summary: "This collection of quotes has been curated from RuPaul's public statements--interviews, books, social media posts, television appearances, and more. The collection includes information on his career, his effect on pop culture, and his perspective on identity, love, and life"-- Provided by publisher.
Identifiers: LCCN 2019034718 (print) | LCCN 2019034719 (ebook) | ISBN 9781572842793 (trade paperback) | ISBN 1572842792 (trade paperback) | ISBN 9781572848375 (ebook) | ISBN 1572848375 (ebook)
Subjects: LCSH: RuPaul, 1960---Quotations. | Television personalities--United States--Quotations. | Female impersonators--United States--Quotations.
Classification: LCC PN1992.4.R86 A25 2020 (print) | LCC PN1992.4.R86 (ebook) | DDC 791.4502/8092--dc23
LC record available at https://lccn.loc.gov/2019034718
LC ebook record available at https://lccn.loc.gov/2019034719

10 9 8 7 6 5 4 3 2 1   20 21 22 23 24

B2 Books is an imprint of Agate Publishing. Agate books are available in bulk at discount prices. For more information, go to agatepublishing.com.

When you become the image of your own imagination, it's the most political thing you can do. When you decide to become a drag queen, which is contrary to everything this male-dominated culture is about, it is the most rebellious act.
—BUZZFEED NEWS, JUNE 2, 2015

Contents

Introduction

EVEN AS A CHILD, RuPaul Charles knew that he was destined for fame. Though he didn't know he would become the world's preeminent drag queen or star in an Emmy-winning TV series that would launch multiple spin-offs and countless drag careers, the young RuPaul held a singular conviction: "I knew that I would be famous and I knew that I would be a star." Raised by a single mom in San Diego's tract housing, RuPaul was a dreamer from an early age, a sensitive boy who surrounded himself with others who could "speak [his] language."

At 15, RuPaul moved to Atlanta and attended the Northside School of Performing Arts, an experience he credits with shaping what would become his stage persona. He later began performing on Atlanta public access television, and during that time, a chance performance in drag transformed not only the way others saw him but the way he saw himself. RuPaul worked the Atlanta club scene, but he was no overnight success. "Everything about Ru's career has been a slow rise," says friend and producer Randy Barbato. This period, which RuPaul characterizes as "not officially drag yet" but rather "punk or gender fuck," was a crucial stage in his artistic evolution. During this time, he formed relationships that would sustain him throughout his career and honed his triple-threat talents as a singer, dancer, and performer.

RuPaul moved to New York in the mid-1980s, working as a go-go dancer and performing at the annual drag festival Wigstock. With the release of his first single, "Supermodel (You Better Work)," in 1992, he experienced his first taste of international fame. Two years later, he was asked to be a spokesmodel for MAC Cosmetics, making him the first drag queen to become the face of a major cosmetics campaign. He continued making TV and film appearances throughout the 1990s, developing his signature glamorous Barbie-blonde drag look, releasing multiple studio albums, and starring in his own talk show.

It was after a nearly eight-year hiatus starting in the late '90s that RuPaul eventually launched what has been his most influential and massively successful project: *RuPaul's Drag Race*. The reality competition show, which crowns one lucky queen "America's Next Drag Superstar," premiered in 2009 to a small audience, but the show's viewership grew by word of mouth, and it soon became a cultural phenomenon.

It is difficult to overstate the impact that the show has had in bringing awareness of drag to mainstream America over 11 seasons and counting. The show now boasts multiple spin-offs and Emmy wins and has featured such high-profile guest stars as Diana Ross, Cher, and Lady Gaga. The show has also firmly positioned RuPaul as the reigning queen of drag queens, as he has helped launch the careers of the more than 100 contestants who have competed on the show.

While *Drag Race* has done an enormous amount to centralize the LGBTQ experience in American popular culture, RuPaul's relationship with the LGBTQ community has, at times, been controversial, and those controversies have reflected the evolution of the LGBTQ community over the decade since the show's premiere. RuPaul came under fire in 2018 when he stated in an interview that he "probably" would not allow a transgender contestant who had begun the process of transitioning to compete on *Drag Race*, and then followed up with an ill-advised tweet doubling down on his position. Shortly after, he recanted his statement and indicated he had much to learn from the transgender community. More recently, he has expressed an openness to learn from contestants on the show and evolve as times change: "Every season the girls come and they challenge me," he says.

Not surprisingly for a drag queen, transformation is a major theme throughout RuPaul's body of work. He consistently emphasizes the power of drag to expand one's consciousness, speaking of drag's power to upend notions of identity: "We're all born naked and the rest is drag," he is fond of saying. RuPaul—"Mama Ru," as his legions of fans affectionately call him—cites Oprah Winfrey as one of his heroes, and in many ways, at 59 years old, RuPaul occupies a similar cultural position to Oprah as both a spiritual and business guru. (*GuRu*, not coincidentally, is the title of his third book.)

His latest project, a revamped version of his mid-'90s talk show, *RuPaul*, seems a fitting platform to showcase the wisdom earned over a long career. RuPaul credits his longevity in show business to both flexibility and perseverance, and he shows no signs of slowing down. "I don't turn down jobs. I will work until I can't work no more," he said in May 2019. The same tenacity that drove the sensitive young boy growing up in San Diego is, it seems, still driving RuPaul today.

Part I

BEGINNINGS

Early Life and Family

MY MOTHER GOT the name out of Ebony magazine. It was spelled Ripoll, but she's Creole, so she made it into this saucy, Frenchy concoction. I always teased her that with a name like RuPaul Andre Charles, I could have either gotten into show business or become a hairdresser. So I chose both.

—*Washington Post*, September 17, 1993

I'M BORN IN 1960 and I lived in San Diego. It was, it's still, very gorgeous there. You could easily have an age of innocence there, and I did, sort of.

—*It Got Better*, June 3, 2015

AT 12, I decided to live my life as if it were a made for TV movie, starring me in every scene.

—Twitter, July 18, 2012

I've been a daydreamer since day one. I much prefer looking out a window over looking at my phone.

—*GuRu*, October 23, 2018

I WAS A sweet, sweet little boy, very kind, very well-mannered, and misunderstood because I always saw many colors in the rainbow and a lot of people feel threatened by that. A lot of people have a vested interest in not seeing the colors because they don't want to remember who they really are. It's too much for them.

—*InnerVIEWS*, **March 17, 2011**

PEOPLE WEREN'T NECESSARILY mean to me, I wasn't necessarily bullied or anything, but they didn't know what to do, they felt uncomfortable. That's why I would put them at ease with a dance, a song, a joke.

—*It Got Better*, **June 3, 2015**

FLIP WILSON'S TELEVISION show was a smash hit, and really for one reason: he would play Geraldine. This character Geraldine, in drag, had everybody tuning in every week. I just can't stress how big a cultural phenomenon this was.

—*It Got Better*, **June 3, 2015**

MY SISTER HAD a picture of Sylvester on the wall. I said, "Who's that?" She told me who he was—the Cockettes, this radical group of drag queens from San Francisco who would put on these shows. They were an extension of sort of the free love movement, but they were even further beyond that, with beards and glitter in their beards and taking it to that next level. And that is part of that time, it's after the '60s and going into the '70s. You know, it was like, how far can we take the sexual revolution, the cultural revolution?

—It Got Better, June 3, 2015

I WENT OUT searching for people who could speak my language. And luckily for me my sister Renetta, who's seven years older than me, she speaks it. She speaks it not as broad, but she was the closest I could come to having someone to take care of me.

—InnerVIEWS, March 17, 2011

I knew I had a personality, had something that I thought had value, I just didn't know specifically what language or what venue it would be.

—*Rolling Stone*, October 4, 2013

MY OLDER SISTER reminds me all the time that I was running around the backyard in her clothes as soon as I could walk. I wasn't thinking "this is drag," I was thinking "this is fun."

—*GuRu*, October 23, 2018

I KNEW THAT I would be famous and I knew that I would be a star, but I knew I couldn't go directly to Los Angeles. . . . I'm telling you, I knew this at 12 years old.

—*E! News*, November 17, 2018

[MY PARENTS] WERE people who never should have been together. These were people, I think, probably should never have had children, maybe had children for all the wrong reasons. Whatever, but we're here, it's fine. But it was not something that you'd want little babies to go through. But it made us all very strong.

—*InnerVIEWS*, March 17, 2011

[My mother] was a bad bitch. Everyone in the neighborhood called her Mean Miss Charles, and I said, **"No, she's not mean, she's just direct."**

—*Rolling Stone*, October 4, 2013

Above all, [my mother] was my ultimate inspiration because **she was the first drag queen I ever saw**.

—*Lettin' It All Hang Out*, June 6, 1996

MY PARENTS WERE batshit crazy. It was fighting and hostility. I wrote about this time that my mother poured gasoline all over my father's car. It's parked in the garage of our family house and she's standing over it saying, "Mother-f, I will light this bitch up." I remember the fire trucks coming. It was this huge scene. And when I remember the scene back, I'm like a camera outside of myself, looking at the scene and sort of surveying, panning the whole scene.

—It Got Better, June 3, 2015

THE ONLY WAY for me to deal with the trauma of what was going on was for me to disconnect and detach from my emotions and my feelings, which is *not* a good thing for kids. That is a *terrible* thing. So the way that we were able to get through that was to laugh.

—It Got Better, June 3, 2015

MY FAMILY LIFE was tumultuous—crazy hillbilly people. It was a war zone.

—Buzzfeed News, June 2, 2015

I REMEMBER WHEN I was five years old . . .
[my mother] said, "Ru, you are too goddamn
sensitive." And she was right, by the way. I still
am. I'm *way* too sensitive. But it took me many
years to understand what she was doing to
me. She was trying to get me prepared for the
world because she didn't want for me what had
happened to her.

—**RuPaul's DragCon 2016, May 8, 2016**

THE OFFICIAL CAUSE of death was cancer, but
we all knew that Mama died from a broken
heart. What broke her heart, was the world
broke her heart.

—**RuPaul's DragCon 2016, May 8, 2016**

MY 10TH GRADE teacher told me, "RuPaul, don't
take life too seriously." It was the greatest lesson
I ever learned in school.

—**Vice, October 16, 2016**

I flunked 10th grade & dropped out of high school the following year. **I learned everything I know from watching television.**

—Twitter, September 3, 2018

SAN DIEGO IN the '70s was very white, very conservative. Thirteen, fourteen [was] when I couldn't fake it anymore. I couldn't fake playing dumb anymore or trying to fit in to what I felt like people wanted me to do. I knew that my tribe was out there waiting for me and they were *not* in San Diego.

—*It Got Better*, June 3, 2015

I COULDN'T EXACTLY hide, you know—
I was six foot tall at 16 years old.

—*Washington Post*, September 17, 1993

I KEPT RECREATING the little boy left behind on the porch. I just kept recreating it, until I said, "No, the problem isn't what the world is doing to me. The problem is that I am actually attracted to those situations."

—*On Point*, October 22, 2018

Creative Evolution

IF YOU LOOK at YouTube videos of me from the early '80s, I'm always talking about loving yourself and expressing yourself and learning how to love yourself. I'm still the same.

—*Interview*, September 2, 2013

WHEN I STARTED in bands in Atlanta, everybody in that area had flocked from all over the Southeast to come to Atlanta because the B-52s and R.E.M. had hit it big. So everybody in that area was thinking, well, we'll go to Atlanta, we'll start a band. . . . They asked me to be in the "Love Shack" video, which was 30 years ago by the way, and I had just come from up in the club, so I was wearing the same thing I'd been up in the club in. I'm wearing it up in the video.

—BUILD Series, June 6, 2019

I VOWED TO get to [*The American Music Show* on public access TV] by any means necessary, and sent in a picture of myself and a letter saying that I'd like to be on the show. One day while I was home Paul Burke called me and invited me on the show. I couldn't believe he was calling me, because in my mind he was a star. Meanwhile they couldn't believe I had written them a letter. When they read it they were falling about screaming, "Oh, my God, somebody wants to be on our show."

—*Lettin' It All Hang Out*, **June 6, 1996**

I CAN ALWAYS come back home again, and Atlanta's just my home, this is where I belong, you know? I have to come back here to get my battery energized and stuff.

—*The American Music Show*, **1992**

I miss the Atlanta that I lived in. That Atlanta is long gone. It's like a childhood friend who underwent head to toe plastic surgery and who I don't recognize anymore.

—WikiNews, October 6, 2007

As TIME WENT on and bills needed to be paid, I shaved them legs and went to Lady Foot Locker, put some socks up in a bra, and history was made, baby. And I moved to New York with a pair of high heels and a dream, hello.

—**BUILD Series, June 6, 2019**

I WAS TRIPPING yesterday morning—just tripping on life—and I realized that I'm doing a lot of the thinking for other people that they don't have time to do, because they're busy working or doing something else.

—***The American Music Show*, February 21, 1985**

I moved to NYC with a pair of high heels and a dream.

The heels were a size too small, but my dream was bigger than the whole Tri-State.

—Twitter, December 30, 2013

ALL OF THE artists, performers, and wannabes who had flocked to New York City in my generation had all come to fulfill the Warhol fantasy. We came to claim our fifteen minutes of fame and live like the bohemian rock stars we'd read about in the magazines.

—*GuRu*, October 23, 2018

I KNEW THAT, in my heart of hearts, that I'd have to go to New York first and *then* come to Hollywood. Because I thought, "I will go to New York, create a persona for myself, and then Hollywood will beckon."

—*It Got Better*, June 3, 2015

MY FIRST 10 yrs in "the biz" I barely made rent money, but I hung in there because I knew that show business was my destiny, child.

—Twitter, May 8, 2012

THERE WAS A window of opportunity that opened, it was very clear. We had been leading up to that. Also, politically, Clinton was in office and the Democrats had sort of this social way of thinking had come into our consciousness collectively and it felt right.

—*InnerVIEWS*, March 17, 2011

I STARTED IN show business professionally in '82 and then "Supermodel" came out in '92, so those 10,000 hours, if you will, those were my college years. Those were the years when I put in the hard yards.

—BUILD Series, June 6, 2019

BUT, EVEN AS a kid, I've always admired and taken my fashion aesthetic from the world of prostitution. I always loved what prostitutes wear. In the 80s my look was a combination of street-walker and soul train dancer, but my WHORE commercial was totally inspired by the working girls on the West Side Highway in New York at that time.

—*Dazed*, June 1, 2015

WE WOULD TERRORIZE the neighborhoods and have a great time doing lots of naughty, naughty things. But I knew that those days were over as soon as I got the news [about the March on Washington for Lesbian, Gay, and Bi Equal Rights and Liberation], because it was clear I had to represent a faction of society that had gone unnoticed and didn't have a voice.

—E! News, **November 17, 2018**

I DIDN'T MAKE any real money until my early thirties. Up until then I had been living from hand to mouth working in nightclubs. My first bit of real coinage came when I got an advance on my recording contract.

—Workin' It! RuPaul's Guide to Life, Liberty, and the Pursuit of Style, **February 2, 2010**

WHEN I WAS ready to go mainstream, I took the sexualized raunchiness out. The glamazon supermodel was a caricature that you could bring home to meet Mom and Dad. I was well-spoken. I was Miss Black America.

—E! News, **November 17, 2018**

I didn't set out to be a role model, I set out to be a supermodel, can I get an amen up in here?

—BUILD Series, June 6, 2019

MY 20'S WERE filled with so much self-doubt and ppl pleasing.

—**Twitter, December 1, 2015**

YOU WANT TO know the truth about drugs? You can only go one or two ways. You can go up, or you can go down. That's it. After a certain point, though, no matter what you do, what you take, you don't go anywhere, and that's when you've got to sit down and face yourself.

—*Lettin' It All Hang Out*, **June 6, 1996**

I QUIT DRINKING, quit doing drugs, and I started to take care of myself. . . . And once I had made *that* decision, the fear melted away. I wasn't scared anymore. I didn't know what lay ahead, but whatever it was I was doing the right thing, so I knew that one way or another I would make it.

—*Lettin' It All Hang Out*, **June 6, 1996**

THERE CAME A time in '99 where I thought, you know what? I'm gonna step back for a minute. An artist steps away from the canvas. I intuitively, instinctively knew it was time to step away.

—**BUILD Series, June 6, 2019**

Part II

SELF

Identity

ONCE I FIGURED out what people were doing and what society was doing, I realized: I don't want to fit into that. I want to stay on the outside of that.

—**NPR, February 2, 2012**

I NEVER HAD to "come out," because I was never "in." It was understood that Ru was Ru.

—*Vogue*, **April 15, 2019**

I IDENTIFY AS nothing.

—**Twitter, June 16, 2015**

SAY IT WITH me, you are everything and nothing at all.

—**BUILD Series, June 6, 2019**

IT DON'T MATTER, baby, just so long as you call me. You can call me he, you can call me she, or you can call me Regis and Kathie Lee.

—*Rolling Stone*, **August 5, 1993**

I'd rather boogie than try to fit in.

—Twitter, October 27, 2015

I've ALWAYS MAINTAINED that we are all actors on a stage and that we play these roles we inherit from society. But if you're able to see that and recognize that it's all an illusion, you have the upper hand in creating where your character can go.

—GuRu, **October 23, 2018**

I NEVER FORGET the fact that I am a spiritual being having a human experience.... It's such a, pardon the pun, drag to deal with, all of that human stuff.

—Curve, **January 20, 2009**

I've BEEN SHUNNED by whites for being black, by blacks for being gay, and by gays for being fem. The real tee? The ego needs to feel superior over others.

—GuRu, **October 23, 2018**

PEOPLE HAVE ALWAYS been threatened by me as an African-American man, because of the inherent black rage that all black people have in our culture, the underlying black rage because of what happened to us in this country.

—*Guardian*, March 3, 2018

BEING A BLACK person in this country, we're always very sensitive about, "Oh my goodness, is this going to be another put-down situation? Am I going to be rejected in this situation?" And I had to work through that and I couldn't carry that hurt with me anymore.

—*On Point*, October 22, 2018

OTHER PEOPLE ARE going to talk shit about you. But what other people have to say about you ain't none of your goddamn business.

—*Billboard*, March 10, 2016

Assimilate? Bitch, please. I'd rather drink muddy water and sleep in a hollow log.

—Twitter, March 13, 2015

See, I'm yin-yang, the whole shebang.

—*Washington Post*, September 17, 1993

AT SOME POINT all gay children realize that they are different, out of sync or set apart from what everyone else is doing. I think this happens sooner rather than later—years before you have any idea what sex is or who Liza Minnelli is.

—*Lettin' It All Hang Out*, June 6, 1996

EVERYBODY'S LIKE, "Oh my god, I'm offended!" It's an ego-based culture we live in. The ego has everything to do with identity. So, you know, drag actually mocks identity.

—*Huffington Post*, January 14, 2012

YOU KNOW, THE matrix says, "Pick an identity and stick with it. Because I want to sell you some beer and shampoo and I need you to stick with what you are so I'll know how to market it to you." Drag is the opposite. Drag says, "Identity is a joke."

—*ABC News*, May 12, 2016

I'M VERY HAPPY with being a big old black man. It's just, I'm an entertainer. I've done lots of different personas. But this one, baby, this one clicks. The children respond to me in drag, OK?

—*The Arsenio Hall Show*, May 28, 1993

I'M BI-CURIOUS, SO I live in both New York and Los Angeles.

—LA Made, June 25, 2017

WHEN I'M TALKING about myself with, say, my manager or other business associates in mixed company, like in a restaurant, rather than say my name, I will say, "Oh, the Monster," you know.

—*InnerVIEWS*, March 17, 2011

MY PURPOSE IS to really have fun, live my life and do as much as I can while I have this fabulous, gorgeous body.

—*Marketplace*, October 23, 2018

Quick Reminder: **Everyone is faking it.**

—Twitter, December 5, 2014

When you're a shape-shifter, you understand that your true self is actually God in drag.

—*Billboard*, March 10, 2016

Relationships

43

Our biggest misconception is that we think we're separate from one another.

—Twitter, May 27, 2018

[MY FATHER] WOULDN'T show up. And through years of therapy, all roads lead to that one moment. And I created an identity around that hurt.

—*On Point*, October 22, 2018

MY FATHER WAS a damaged person. He was damaged by society, black rage, and so to key into my frequency of love and saying, "I love you so much" would force him to get in touch with his own feelings, which he couldn't. It was too dangerous for him to do it.

—*On Point*, October 22, 2018

THE FIRST HALF of my career was really about getting my father's attention.

—*On Point*, October 22, 2018

AFTER YEARS OF analyzing & deconstructing my father, I finally concluded that he was mostly a figment of my imagination.

—Twitter, July 13, 2018

You need
those friends
who are going
to shake you
up and say,
"Dorothy, wake
up" when you
get stuck in the
poppy field.

—*E! News*, November 17, 2018

YOU HAVE TO understand the African American male in our society—where he's coming from and how he had to get over using what he knew, the best he could. Ike Turner is my father, you know? And I forgive him, I understand where he's coming from, even though it's not where I'm coming from. We have to learn how to love him, and we have to learn how to teach him how to love himself, because he obviously doesn't.

—Rolling Stone, **August 5, 1993**

MY FOLKS, AND other folks in the South, had such traumatic experiences. I was able to dissect and deconstruct some of my feelings. I could afford to do it. They couldn't afford to do it.

—New York Times, **January 24, 2018**

I'M SO PROUD that I can share this with my family. So many children can't go home—some kids can't go home because their family won't accept them. And hopefully by me coming out and being who I am, I can shed some light on what the lifestyle is like, which is just like anybody else.

—The Arsenio Hall Show, **May 28, 1993**

I LOVE MY sisters. They're great, but the people on my path, like the Scarecrow, the Tin Man, and the Cowardly Lion, they're the ones who I have forged this life with, this real bond. They've allowed me to be who I am in a way that my first family really couldn't. They did initially, but I moved on.

—*Vanity Fair*, March 13, 2017

THROUGHOUT MY CAREER, I've relied on a handful of people who have always had my best interests at heart. People whom I love and trust. And who can offer me a unique perspective that I can't always see on my own.

—*GuRu*, October 23, 2018

I LOVE TO laugh, and [longtime friend and drag queen Lady] Bunny is the funniest person I've ever met—really.

—*Interview*, September 2, 2013

It's the most amazing thing I have ever done in my life, is allow someone to love me.

—*New York Times* video, May 6, 2013

[MY PARTNER, GEORGES LEBAR, IS] so kind and funny. I remember praying, "I want a sweet, sensitive man," and I got an Australian who's just lovely.

—**Buzzfeed News, June 2, 2015**

[GEORGES LEBAR] WAS on the dance floor dancing like a maniac. I had to go over and say, "What are you going through?"

—*E! News*, **November 17, 2018**

HE AND I are very respectful of one another. He and I know that on this planet where there are millions and millions of people, the person I have found on this planet that I like the very most is him. And I know that for him the person he loves the most on this planet is me. I know that; there's no doubt in my mind. So if he needs to do something else somewhere else, I'm fine with that.

—*Guardian*, **March 3, 2018**

THAT [MARRIAGE] PAPER don't mean nothing.
If you're devoted to a person, nothing's gonna
change that. And after 23 years, hey, I know him,
he knows me, I love him. He's my favorite person
on the planet I've met.

—*Entertainment Tonight*, March 15, 2017

THIS CONCEPT OF marriage that we were
raised with is so different from the real style of
relationships that linger for years and years.

—*Entertainment Tonight*, March 15, 2017

I'VE HAD SEX, I've enjoyed sex, it's not that
important to me.

—*Rolling Stone*, October 4, 2013

Got no time to H8 the people who H8 me, too busy loving the people who love me.

—Twitter, September 1, 2016

IT's PERFECTLY FINE to say "I actually don't want to talk about my love because that's not part of the fantasy world I created in commerce."

—*Toronto Sun*, July 2, 2016

MY GOAL IS to always come from a place of love, but sometimes I just have to break it down for a motherf%ker.

—Twitter, June 23, 2013

AVOID DUMB PEOPLE. Do not try to educate them or try to prove how superior you are to them. Just smile and stay away from them.

—Twitter, February 17, 2019

If your happiness is contingent on someone else changing their behavior, then you playin yo'self, henny.

—Twitter, May 4, 2015

Fame

WELL, WHEN MY mother was pregnant with me
she had seen a psychic who told her that you're
carrying a boy and this boy will be famous. So
I grew up knowing I was going to be famous.
I didn't know how I was going to be famous,
but I knew I would be famous.

—*Marketplace*, October 23, 2018

NEWTOFAME101: Becoming famous is a lot
like getting drunk on booze; you never know if
someone is gonna be a fun drunk or a mean drunk.

—**Twitter, June 7, 2015**

NEWTOFAME101: Show up on time,
be prepared and don't complain.

—**Twitter, May 7, 2015**

WANNA "MAKE IT" in show biz? First, ask
yourself how much humiliation heartbreak
rejection and sacrifice are you willing to endure?

—**Twitter, August 5, 2015**

NewToFame101:
Keep in mind
that your younger
replacement just
arrived at the bus
terminal.

—Twitter, May 7, 2015

NEVER FORGET: One wrong move and your audience will turn and burn you at the stake.

—Twitter, March 15, 2015

HARD WORK TO get "big break," even harder to maintain for 23yrs. My job is more demanding today than it EVER was.

—Twitter, December 16, 2015

IF YOU'RE GONNA get into show business, change your name, because you don't want it on public records and police records and things like that.

—*Alan Carr: Chatty Man*, May 29, 2015

[MY STALKER] HAD a tattoo with my name on one leg and she had Cher's name on the other leg so I was in good company.

—Vice, October 16, 2016

TWITTER101: Never respond to trolls, they feed on any attention good or bad. Just block'em.

—Twitter, May 11, 2015

Well, you know, I've been in show business for just under 300 years.

—BUILD Series, May 12, 2016

LET ME TELL you something: I heard the world say my name and I've seen my face on the covers of magazines, and it didn't fulfill me.... The glaring flaw in the success-equals-happiness principle is that it measures everyone by the same superficial assumption that wholeness can be found in material things.

—*Workin' It! RuPaul's Guide to Life, Liberty, and the Pursuit of Style*, February 2, 2010

FAME IS CLEARLY our society's most valued currency. I really wish the media would stop printing the names of mass murderers.

—**Twitter, July 24, 2015**

I'D RATHER HAVE an enema than have an Emmy.

—**Vulture, March 23, 2016**

ON SOCIAL MEDIA I get a lot of people writing to me saying, "Why won't you notice me?" I wanna write them back and say, "Me noticing you will never satisfy your deep craving unless you notice you first."

—*GuRu*, October 23, 2018

As a kid I used my idols as a guide, but when I reached my goal I didn't need them anymore.

—**Twitter, October 21, 2011**

I never set out to become a role model or a trailblazer. My mission was simply to explore life and clear a path within myself to allow the frequency to move through me.

—*GuRu*, **October 23, 2018**

I never set out to be a role model, I may have set out to be a *super* model, but not a role model.

—**British *Vogue*, January 25, 2018**

Thank you for being so kind and lovely all these years. I don't take it for granted.

—**Twitter, September 7, 2015**

Part III

INSPIRATION AND CREATIVITY

Drag

You're born naked and **the rest is drag.**

—*GuRu*, October 23, 2018

I am a drag queen. I don't have to explain myself. My frequency is very common, **and it's open to anybody who wants to tune in**.

—*New York Times*, July 11, 1993

MY MOTIVATION COMES from a love of being creative. I'm in love with music and colour and laughter and dancing and all things that are beautiful.

—Independent, **August 1, 2015**

MY PASSION IS creativity. Drag allows me to be creative on many different levels.

—Twitter, October 1, 2015

CREATIVITY TODAY IS a kind of shopping process—picking up on and sampling things from the world around you, things you grew up with. That's very much my modus operandi. If you knew all the references, you could deconstruct one of my performances and place every look, every word, and every move.

—Lettin' It All Hang Out, **June 6, 1996**

Drag is a miracle.

—*Marketplace*, October 23, 2018

SOMETHING ABOUT A drag queen
commands respect.

WELL, DRAG WILL always exist because it is
really an enlightened state. That's why, you
know, some of the gods in different religions have
always had that duality.

DRAG [QUEENS AND KINGS] have always been the
myth keepers of every culture, the witch doctors,
the shamans. And people who have elevated to
a higher level of consciousness understand that
we are a microcosm of the whole universe, so the
whole universe is both male, female, black, white,
in, out—and that's what we are.

DRAG CAN HELP you understand what you are,
how amazing it is to have a human body, and
what you can do with it.

ANYBODY WHO'S EVER decided they're going
to leave the house in high heels, lipstick and a
plastic wig on their head, you know, and they're
a boy, is so courageous and it takes so much
chutzpah to do that.

—*Curve*, January 20, 2009

DRAG IS MORE than just wanting to dress like a
woman. Drag has everything to do with being a
shape-shifter, and feeling free enough to try all
the colors and not be limited by other people's
opinions.

—*Interview*, September 2, 2013

DRAG ISN'T JUST a man wearing false eyelashes
and a pussycat wig. Drag isn't just a woman with a
pair of glued-on sideburns and an Elvis jumpsuit.
Drag is everything. I don't differentiate drag from
dressing up or dressing down. Whatever you put
on after you get out of the shower is your drag.

—*Workin' It! RuPaul's Guide to Life, Liberty,
and the Pursuit of Style*, February 2, 2010

Doing drag in a male-dominant culture is an act of treason. **It's the most punk-rock thing you can do.**

—*Rolling Stone*, October 4, 2013

Drag ain't for sissies. You've got to toughen up.

—*ABC News*, May 12, 2016

I NEVER THINK of it as women's clothing;
I think of it as drag.

—Independent, August 1, 2015

THERE WAS REALLY never a sense of
impersonating a woman. If anything, it had
more to do with a critique of our culture. You
know, being the only boy in an all-girl family,
I've always been intrigued with looking under
the hood, psychologically, of our culture and
deconstructing femininity or beauty or all that
stuff, so dressing in drag the first time really
had more to do with being told not to do it. So it
was sort of my punk-rock statement to say, "You
know what? F you." You know? And then, from
there, I became addicted to the power it gave me.

—InnerVIEWS, March 17, 2011

DRAG LOSES ITS sense of danger and its sense
of irony once it's not men doing it, because at
its core it's a social statement and a big f-you to
male-dominated culture. So for men to do it, it's
really punk rock, because it's a real rejection of
masculinity.

—Guardian, March 3, 2018

I THINK EVERYBODY likes to toy with their image. I love those guys. I love Milton Berle and Flip Wilson and all those people. I love Barney and Big Bird; they're totally drag queens, too.

—*Rolling Stone*, **August 5, 1993**

IN MY YEARS of doing drag, I realized that there's one common thing with men, and it's that men will stick it in anything. It doesn't matter. They'll say other things when they're, you know, with their family and friends, but when they're alone, any man, I'm talking all men, will stick it in anything.

—*Alan Carr: Chatty Man*, **May 29, 2015**

WE'RE ALL IN drag, and the point of drag is to point that out.

—**BUILD Series, June 6, 2019**

It shows people that everything's temporary. It's just clothes, paint, powder. Drag is like fame: It doesn't hide you. **It reveals who you are.**

—*O, The Oprah Magazine*, January 16, 2018

THESE PERSONAS WE put on, you know, I'm a banker, I'm a basketball coach, or I'm a news presenter, we get too caught up in what that means and it becomes too heavy. So if you understand it's just like an outfit that you wear, like drag, it helps you navigate this world.

—**NowThis News, October 25, 2018**

THE DRAG CREED, really, is, *Do not take life too—* capital letters, "TOO"—*f—ing seriously*.

—***Time*, June 12, 2017**

WE DO NOT stand on ceremony, and we do not take words seriously. We do take feelings seriously and intention seriously, and the intention is not to be hateful at all.

—**Vulture, March 23, 2016**

FOR THE SWEET sensitive souls who have been disenfranchised by the world, it's the irreverence, it's the laughter that keeps us going.

—***What's the Tee?*, December 14, 2016**

WE MOCK IDENTITY. They [the trans community] take identity very seriously. So it's the complete opposite ends of the scale. To a layperson, it seems very similar, but it's really not.

—**Vulture, March 23, 2016**

GAY MEN DON'T do drag to mock women, we do drag to mock the cultural concept of identity. If you don't get irony, you don't get drag.

—**Twitter, May 9, 2016**

IT'S ALL NUDGE, nudge, wink, wink, wink. We never believe this is who we are. That is why drag is a revolution, because we're mocking identity. We're mocking everyone.

—***New York Times**, January 24, 2018*

DRAG HAS ALWAYS been off-the-grid.

—***Independent**, August 1, 2015*

As drag queens, it's our job to mock the hypocrisy, mediocrity, and absurdity of society.

—*GuRu*, October 23, 2018

I ALWAYS THOUGHT it was quite obvious that my approach to drag is more wink-wink than the "look-and-feel-of-real."

—*Workin' It! RuPaul's Guide to Life, Liberty, and the Pursuit of Style*, February 2, 2010

FISHINESS ALLUDES TO the look and feel of "real." For most drag queens, that's not the criteria. Because the look and feel of real is boring.

—Vulture, March 23, 2016

EVEN BEFORE I knew what my sexuality was, people told me, "You look like a little girl." And being that "thing" I've always been able to hear what the universe was telling me: "Ru, you would look great in a blond wig and a pair of Frederick's of Hollywood pumps."

—*New York Times*, July 11, 1993

I wanted to be David Bowie but the universe said, **"Bitch, you are a drag queen."**

—BUILD Series, June 6, 2019

SEEING MYSELF TRANSFORMED is such a trip. I've never gotten used to seeing myself in drag. Or out of drag for that matter. I've always felt like The Boy Who Fell to Earth and landed in this body.

—*GuRu*, **October 23, 2018**

WHEN I GOT into drag, straight men, straight women, everybody would go, "Bitch, *damn*." And I could feel it. I had never felt it before. I knew I had power. And I knew that it was important for me to get a lot of work done, wherever I was.

—*E! News*, **November 17, 2018**

[DRAG] WAS A great social commentary, and people responded to me in drag like I never experienced before.

—*Rolling Stone*, **October 4, 2013**

MY DRAG HAS confused people—and please do not hear this the wrong way—my drag has confused people because I look so goddamn good. Most people miss the message, which is it's not something to be taken seriously.

—*It Got Better*, **June 3, 2015**

DURING THE LATTER part of the eighties, I transformed my look to accommodate a change in the nightclub business. To make money from hosting parties and go-go dancing gigs, I became a sexy drag queen. Up till then, my repertoire of looks consisted of "funky downtown bohemian" and "gender f@&k."

—*Workin' It! RuPaul's Guide to Life, Liberty, and the Pursuit of Style*, February 2, 2010

[THE REAGAN-ERA NEW YORK DRAG SCENE] was social commentary. It was wearing ratty wigs and combat boots and big old water balloon falsies and saying, "Look at me, I'm just as freaky as any Reaganomic Tipper Gore nightmare."

—*New York Times*, July 11, 1993

MY DRAG LOOK has had several incarnations, but the one that became my signature look was conceived by the marketing man in me. I wanted a recognizable silhouette that could be easily drawn by a caricature artist and emulated by a sketch comedy troupe.

—*GuRu*, October 23, 2018

IT WAS A calculated effort to take sexuality out of my image. It was more like a Disney caricature, rather than a sexualized, subversive character.

—*Interview*, **September 2, 2013**

IN MY CAREER, I've been able to show certain angles. I've been able to paint on a face and edit what I presented.

—*Vogue*, **April 15, 2019**

MY HAIRSTYLES ARE heavy as hell and always consist of two wigs. And yes, bruising, welts, and some scarring can occur after five weeks of fourteen-hour days in drag. I thought you knew— drag ain't for sissies!

—*Workin' It! RuPaul's Guide to Life, Liberty, and the Pursuit of Style*, **February 2, 2010**

[ON HOW LONG it takes him to get into drag] About 300 years. I started right after the Second World War.

—*Jimmy Kimmel Live*, **December 3, 2018**

I love getting ready; it's like a meditation.

I shave my whole body. If you can find a human hair on my body, I'll give you a hundred bucks.

—*Rolling Stone*, August 5, 1993

BUT IF THE eyebrows don't fit your face, if the curve isn't quite right, the rest is useless—unless you're going for the look of a snaggle-toothed hag, which is a look that I have found useful in the past.

—Lettin' It All Hang Out, **June 6, 1996**

TUCKING IS A delicate procedure that I have described as an ancient Chinese secret. On other occasions I have said that I am "sitting on a secret," and that's really it in a nutshell.

—Lettin' It All Hang Out, **June 6, 1996**

I TOLD MY therapist that I used to feel like Superman in drag, to my everyday Clark Kent. Now the only difference is I *always* have that power.

—Rolling Stone, **October 4, 2013**

[Drag] actually didn't save my life, it gave me a life. I don't think there is a life in the mundane 9-to-5 hypocrisy. **That's not living. That's just part of the Matrix.**

—Vulture, March 23, 2016

MY PRESENCE IN the pop landscape has allowed people to see themselves as their superhero. Drag for me has always been my superhero costume.

—GuRu, **October 23, 2018**

MY DRAG PERSONA sort of sucks the air out of the room. You know what I mean? It's larger than life, and it would make you probably feel uncomfortable, darling.

—Alan Carr: Chatty Man, **May 29, 2015**

MY ABILITY TO cross over has to do with cultural changes but also a scientific approach to creating a persona that doesn't threaten people. My persona is only dangerous in broad strokes.

—Independent, **August 1, 2015**

Because I am not the sole and exclusive author of this process, I have been able to watch it one step removed. That's why I often think of myself in the third person, not because I think I am royal—although I am a queen—but because I see RuPaul as a product. The RuPaul experience is rather like a ride in a theme park: You put a quarter in the slot and off I go.

—*Lettin' It All Hang Out*, June 6, 1996

I like to refer to myself as an enter-*taint*-er.

—BUILD Series, May 12, 2016

The only time people ever see me in drag anymore is if I'm on television. But I gotta say, years ago before I got famous, it was so much fun. But once I got famous it became a real job.

—*Alan Carr: Chatty Man*, May 29, 2015

The only time you'll see me in drag now is if I'm getting paid a load of money.

—*Independent*, August 1, 2015

It's not who I am, it's what I do for a living.

—*Marketplace*, October 23, 2018

IF I NEVER go drag again after today, I don't care. It's not that important to me. It never was.

—Rolling Stone, October 4, 2013

CONFESSION: I'VE NEVER worn a costume on Halloween (but try catching me OUT of one the other 364 days of the year).

—Twitter, October 23, 2011

ANYTHING TO DO with gender experimentation in a fear-based period of time has to go underground because it's too scary for people when they're doing the fear thing. So re-introducing drag to a younger generation I thought was important for me, for my legacy, too.

—Curve, January 20, 2009

What you're witnessing with drag is the most mainstream it will get.

—Vulture, March 23, 2016

THIS GENERATION—AND WE see this with DragCon, which we're doing in New York September 9 and 10—young, young people, we're talking 12, 13, 14, they are carrying the torch. They are identifying as gender fluid, even if they don't know what that really means, and they're understanding that they are our salvation. They will not let this movement die. And it has less to do with dressing in drag, but more to do with the freedom of expression and the ability to choose how they see themselves in the world.

—*Time*, June 12, 2017

THERE IS AN aspect, a superficial aspect, of drag that *is* mainstream, where people are saying, "Ooo, she threw me shade," and, "Ooo, work it girl," or, "Ooo, she is giving me lots of gags." I don't know if people say that, but it seems like something people might say, you know, in the mainstream. I wouldn't know. . . . But the deeper meaning of drag is lost on most people.

—BUILD Series, June 6, 2019

Fashion and Beauty

I've always said that it's best to look your best when you feel your worst.

—*Grazia*, June 1, 2015

I AM THE Queen of Queens, and the Queen of Queens deserves to look, is expected to look, like a million dollars.

—Marketplace, **October 23, 2018**

THE SIGNATURE LOOK, you know, it's like asking Coca-Cola, are you going to change the formula? I don't think so.

—NPR, February 2, 2012

THE DECISION TO become a full-time blonde came from my desire to create a cartoon character image that could be easily identified as a brand.

—Workin' It! RuPaul's Guide to Life, Liberty, and the Pursuit of Style, **February 2, 2010**

PEOPLE ALWAYS ASK me, "How many wigs do you own?" Truth is, I don't really know. Probably one hundred, but the number of "girls" (as we like to call the wigs) currently in rotation for filming and performances is closer to fifteen.

> —*Workin' It! RuPaul's Guide to Life, Liberty, and the Pursuit of Style*, **February 2, 2010**

BLACK HAIR REALLY is the most fabulous over the top thing that there is. Growing up, the myth was you couldn't do anything with black hair. WRONG.

> —*Lettin' It All Hang Out*, **June 6, 1996**

I CHANGE CLOTHES at least three times a day. It's the only way I can justify all the shopping I do. Prada to the grocery store? Yes! Gucci to the dry cleaner's? Why not? Dolce & Gabbana to the corner deli? I insist!

> —*Workin' It! RuPaul's Guide to Life, Liberty, and the Pursuit of Style*, **February 2, 2010**

It's a cliché, but I think that who you are on the inside shows on your face.

—*Interview*, September 2, 2013

I detest casual clothes.

—Twitter, October 2, 2011

Flats are for quitters.

—*Weekend Edition Sunday*, **January 28, 2018**

I GOT TURNED on to mules by my kindergarten teacher, Miss Garfield, and she drove a Cadillac and wore really sexy clothes.

—Rolling Stone, **August 5, 1993**

ANYONE WHO WEARS false eyelashes between 9am & 5pm is a mother%king genius.

—Twitter, December 13, 2012

ACTUALLY, I'M PROBABLY 99-and-a-half percent plastic now.

—Interview, **September 2, 2013**

Music

I KNEW THAT I could express myself that way, through music stars like David Bowie, and Cher, and Diana Ross, Sylvester. That's where I gravitated. You know, young kids have a hard time articulating what they're feeling, so they gravitate toward pop stars, and they can go, "That right there, that's what I'm feeling right there." And that's why it's young kids who buy music, and then when people learn to articulate, they stop buying music.

—*InnerVIEWS*, March 17, 2011

MUSIC HAS ALWAYS been the place I found my refuge. I was always a weird little kid who would read album cover liners.

—BUILD Series, May 12, 2016

[MUSIC IS] THE physical blood of communication. When I've connected with someone on music, I know them. It's like a shortcut to their intellectual DNA.

—*InnerVIEWS*, March 17, 2011

You have to *live* the song, every breath and every beat. Beyond that it doesn't really matter if you know the words or not.

—Lettin' It All Hang Out, June 6, 1996

Sometimes I reboot my emotional system by listening to a song that makes me cry real hard.

—Twitter, July 25, 2012

WITH TAPES IT'S like jacking off, and with
the live band it's like really fucking.

—The American Music Show, **February 21, 1985**

EARLY ON, I connected with Diana Ross from
the *The Ed Sullivan Show*. You know, there were
three girls up there, but only one of them had that
thing. And I remember . . . hearing "Baby Love"
on the radio and sort of emulating her moves, the
way she scrunched her shoulders up and her big
eyes and her big smile.

—It Got Better, **June 3, 2015**

THERE'S A LONG history of drag and part of that
history is [Gloria Gaynor's "I Will Survive"].
It is like not knowing the words to the national
anthem.

—Los Angeles Times, **August 10, 2016**

IN THE EARLY '70s, it was David Bowie, because
I thought, "This creature, so beautiful." And
everything that I felt on the inside, he was doing
on the outside.

—It Got Better, **June 3, 2015**

THROUGH [BOWIE'S] MUSIC and his art, how he projected this image out there. And it was never cocky. Part of the rock creed is to wear black and cover up and smoke a cigarette and be exclusive. His wasn't that way. His was always open.

—Vulture, March 23, 2016

[MY MUSICAL INFLUENCES ARE] Luther Vandross, Diana Ross and Chaka Khan, but when you hear my album, I don't sound like any of those people!

—*Rolling Stone*, August 5, 1993

RuPaul's Drag Race

I COME FROM a family of teachers. And I knew that I had it in me to be a mentor and to have this show be a portal to helping people find their audience.

—*Huffington Post*, January 14, 2012

WE'RE LOOKING FOR people who are showgirls, not just anyone who owns a pussycat wig and a pair of high heels.

—*Huffington Post*, January 14, 2012

IN THE 10 years we've been casting Drag Race, the only thing we've ever screened for is charisma uniqueness nerve and talent. And that will never change.

—Twitter, March 5, 2018

NINE OUT OF 10 of the people who audition for our show, they'll say these words—and it's funny 'cause we all laugh every time we hear it—they say, "Honey, I will *cut* a bitch!" Nine out of 10! "I will *cut* a bitch!"

—*Vanity Fair*, March 13, 2017

The 25 percent who get through, who are authentic, I fall in love with them, because they reveal themselves.

—*Time*, June 12, 2017

Good luck, and don't fuck it up.

—*RuPaul's Drag Race*

"DRAG RACE" IS popular because at its core it is the story of the tenacity of the human spirit. We get to see these kids who have been pushed aside by society, who've made a way for themselves to be seen and to be great.

—*ABC News*, May 12, 2016

THIS COMPETITION IS designed for a person to break themselves down to their core and build themselves back up again.

—*Time*, June 12, 2017

THE SHOW CHALLENGES the contestants to figuratively die and become reborn into their higher self.

—*On Point*, October 22, 2018

The series, it's all about the tenacity of the human spirit, because queens are some crafty-ass m-fs.

—*Alan Carr: Chatty Man*, May 29, 2015

THE THING IS, we set up the show based on all of the things I've done in my career: morning drive radio, movies, TV, producing, marketing, designing, you name it. Being a pitch person. So all of the challenges were based on everything that I'd done.

—Television Academy Foundation, June 3, 2019

IF I WERE to do Snatch Game, I'm sure that I would impersonate La Toya Jackson.

—BUILD Series, May 12, 2016

THE TIME HAS come to lip-sync for your life.

—*RuPaul's Drag Race*

OH, I DON'T think of [*Lip Sync Battle*]. It's a poor ripoff of our show. Regular, straight pop culture has liberally lifted things from gay culture as long as I can remember. And that's fine, because guess what? We have so much more where that comes from. Take it!

—Vulture, March 23, 2016

We produce the show within an inch of its life.

—*Billboard* Facebook Live, August 16, 2016

I FEEL LIKE a mother-queen-vampire-Dracula because I want to make more girls so I can have more friends and more girls to play with, you know? For a long time, it was really just me.

—*Interview*, **September 2, 2013**

EVERY SEASON THE girls come and they challenge me. A new nose contour technique or a new way to see themselves and identity, and it helps me stay on my game and stay engaged in the conversation.

—*New York Times*, **January 24, 2018**

WHEN I GET all dolled up to film *Drag Race*, I'll take six hours. I could do it in two hours, but it's important for me to make it a deliberately sacred, drawn-out ritual.

—*GuRu*, **October 23, 2018**

THINK ABOUT IT. In all these years that RuPaul has been RuPaul, there's been no b**** who has come for this crown. Year after year, we pick America's next drag superstar. But has she ever come close to Miss RuPaul? I don't think so!

—*All Things Considered*, **August 25, 2016**

I GET THESE young kids who are into drag, and really getting their take about what drag means to them, especially since they've never been through the gay rights movement or the things that I've seen. I'm getting this fresh perspective about drag.

—*New York Times*, August 5, 2011

WE HAVE CONTESTANTS in season 10 who were 10 years old when this show went on television. Or 11 years old. So they are literally the children of *Drag Race*.

—*Hollywood Reporter* video, March 21, 2018

[THE CONTESTANTS] WERE ostracized by their family or society and had to make a way, had to sort of find the light to shine like a lotus in the mud. And in doing so, they are teaching young people how to not only find their tribe but to find their light and to shine in that light.

—*On Point*, October 22, 2018

THAT'S WHY I think our show *Drag Race* is so captivating, because we get to watch these courageous kids that society has thrown away find a way to shine in the light.

—*On Point*, October 22, 2018

I THOUGHT THAT somebody like Jinkx Monsoon winning was so great because he was, in fact, sort of an outsider of an outsider. That's a message that's quite powerful—not only for your viewers, but even within the community.

—*Interview*, September 2, 2013

AND THAT'S THE most exciting thing in working with all of these young people and seeing all these girls come through our show. They're courageous—and they're not afraid of color or of what people have to say or of their bodies. They use their bodies as a tool, as a gift, and I love that.

—*Interview*, September 2, 2013

WHAT WE WEREN'T prepared for was how much heart would come to the surface. You know, in hindsight, of *course* there'd be so much heart. Because these courageous, outrageous, beautiful kids, who society has tossed to the side, who society says, "We have no value in you," these kids are courageous enough to say, "Yeah, great, but I'm gonna do it anyway. I'm gonna make beauty and I'm gonna go for it." When everything in our society says, "You cannot do this," they do it anyway.

—**Television Academy Foundation, June 3, 2019**

WHAT THE SHOW has done on a broad level is really spoken to young people who are out in the middle of nowhere who don't know where their tribe is. To help them identify what they're feeling and who their tribe is, and how to live a life outside of what they were told they're supposed to do. How to successfully live your life without buckling under the pressure of society.

—*All Things Considered*, **August 25, 2016**

If you have a pulse, you can identify with the kids on this show.

—Television Academy Foundation, June 3, 2019

THE TRUTH IS when you try to keep things away from people, it becomes so coveted, they want it so bad. *Especially* young people. And around the world, people for years have been, you know, downloading *Drag Race* in places where they couldn't get it. But that did not stop them.

—BUILD Series, May 12, 2016

ON *DRAG RACE* we've had 100 queens and they have international careers because of the show, so I'm the most proud of the show being a launch pad for their careers. They had careers before but the careers they have now are international and they travel the world, so I'm most proud of that.

—Vice, October 16, 2016

[*DRAG RACE*] DOESN'T have a political agenda in terms of policies in Washington. But it has a position on identity, which is really the most political you can get. It has politics at its core, because it deals with: how do you see yourself on this planet? That's highly political.

—*Guardian*, March 3, 2018

Our goal is to have fun and celebrate the art of drag. If other people can get something out of it or get enlightened from it—right on, ladykins. **But our first objective is to have fun and to entertain.**

—*Weekend Edition Sunday*, January 28, 2018

Part IV

SPEAKING OUT AND SPEAKING PROUD

Conscious-ness Is the New Cool

LEARN TO LOVE yourself. And stay in this moment. This moment right here is where your power is. If you drift into the past or into the future, you lose your power and your ability to love yourself. So this moment right now, be kind and love yourself.

—**NPR, February 2, 2012**

MY SHOW IS about loving yourself and learning how to love yourself. Because if you don't love yourself, how you gonna love somebody else? Can I get an amen in here?

—*The Arsenio Hall Show*, **May 28, 1993**

I LOVE THE book *Animal Farm* because it's about the human experience and how humans forget. The animals in there, they forgot why they had a revolution in the first place. . . . It's like, every morning I wake up, it's like *Groundhog Day*. I forget all over again.

—**BUILD Series, June 6, 2019**

THERE ARE THESE different levels of recognition, right? Kind of like Dorothy in *The Wizard of Oz*, when she looks behind the curtain and goes, "Wait a minute, *you're* the Wiz?" And we have that same experience, we sweet sensitive souls, when we realize that we've been hoaxed by this whole illusion. And the different levels of recognition are, first of all, you're angry. The second level of that recognition is you become cynical, and the next level of that is that it can turn into just straight-up bitterness because you think, "I've been hoaxed, this is all a lie." But most people never get to the next level of recognition, which is the most important level of that recognition, and that level of recognition is joy.

—BUILD Series, June 6, 2019

You are not your circumstances. You can transcend every situation, even—believe it or not— death.

—NPR, February 2, 2012

Every time I tell people to love yourself on television, **I'm actually reminding myself at the same time**.

—*Hollywood Reporter* video, March 21, 2018

THE EGO NEEDS to be recognized. There's this sinking feeling in each of us that we really don't exist. So we go and we create lives on Instagram or we say something provocative on social media so someone gets mad and says, "You, you!" and we're like, "Yeah, tell me more, I must be existing because you're mad at me!"

—BUILD Series, June 6, 2019

IN ESSENCE, THE anaesthesia never worked on me. I always felt like I was awake.

—*Hollywood Reporter* video, March 21, 2018

THE ASSUMPTION IS that if people knew better they would do better, but that's not usually the case. Most people are motivated by subconscious forces that they're not consciously aware of.

—Twitter, June 6, 2018

LOOKING BACK, I realize how much I used smoking to block my feelings and put up a wall around me. Today, I want to feel my feelings. I want to be here for the experience.

—*Workin' It!: RuPaul's Guide to Life, Liberty, and the Pursuit of Style*, February 2, 2010

OVER THE PAST ten years, I've nurtured a
consciousness that lovingly guides me on a day-
to-day, sometimes minute-by-minute, basis. I
recognize this guidance as a kind, loving voice.
It suggests that I keep kindness in my heart, that I
go to the gym, or even that I order a grilled chicken
salad instead of the supersize enchilada combo.

—*Workin' It!: RuPaul's Guide to Life, Liberty,
and the Pursuit of Style*, February 2, 2010

I DON'T DO bitchy. I do sassy. I had been doing
"Everybody say love" since Lord knows when.

—*Lettin' It All Hang Out*, June 6, 1996

I HAVE TO say that when I became an adult and
got out into the world, I thought I was such a
damn freak. But now, having watched a zillion
episodes of *Oprah*, and having heard what other
people's lives are like, I feel quite ordinary.

—*Lettin' It All Hang Out*, June 6, 1996

THE DAY I started loving myself was the
day I became Supermodel of the World.

—*Lettin' It All Hang Out*, June 6, 1996

What other people think of me is not my business.

—WikiNews, October 6, 2007

Throwing shade takes a bit of creativity, being a bitch takes none.

—Twitter, December 7, 2012

IT'S IMPORTANT NOT to dumb yourself down, not to scrunch down, *not to do anything down.*

—Workin' It!: RuPaul's Guide to Life, Liberty, and the Pursuit of Style, February 2, 2010

I DEDICATE THIS Emmy nomination to outsiders everywhere. Brave souls who stick to their dreams and make the world a more colorful place.

—Twitter, July 14, 2016

MOST SWEET SENSITIVE souls use their own intellect against themselves, like the thorns of a rose growing inward.

—Twitter, February 20, 2019

DON'T BELIEVE EVERYTHING U think.

—Twitter, September 11, 2011

VERY EASY TO find participants in a pity party, but can U rock it with the bitches from the bright side?

—Twitter, September 11, 2011

Spirituality

I'VE ALWAYS BEEN aware that I'm a blessed
person. Growing up without a dime to my name,
I knew I always had magic. The ability to turn
any situation into something special.

—GuRu, **October 23, 2018**

YOU ARE NOT who you think you are. This is just
a temporary package that you've put together
on this planet and it's not to be taken seriously.
You're supposed to have fun with it.

—Curve, **January 20, 2009**

HEAVEN OR HELL is a choice I make every
waking second that I'm alive & not something
that happens when I die.

—Twitter, September 10, 2011

YOU ARE NOT this body. You are not your
religion, you are not your politics, you are not
your race, you are not your gender. This is but a
short run on this planet. You go on forever. But
while you're here in this beautiful gift, you've
gotten this role, have fun with it, love it, give love
to somebody, let somebody love you.

—InnerVIEWS, **March 17, 2011**

I am a shapeshifter whose only mission is to experience humanity.

—*GuRu*, October 23, 2018

WE ARE SO incredible. We are an extension of the power that created the whole universe. And we have to acknowledge that and say, "Yes. I am that."

—The Oprah Winfrey Show, 1995

U ARE HEIR to the laws of the world U identify with.

—Twitter, December 18, 2011

MY BIG BREAK was unlocking my own mind's limitations.

—InnerVIEWS, March 17, 2011

PLANET EARTH IS a high school from hell, and we are all just students here.

—Lettin' It All Hang Out, June 6, 1996

A PROBLEM CAN'T truly be solved on the same conscious level it was created on.

—Twitter, December 19, 2011

I hear the voice of my darkness, and I say thanks for sharing, lover, but I'm going to do the opposite of what you're saying.

—*GuRu*, October 23, 2018

EVERY MORNING I wake up, it feels like my tail grows back. And I have to recenter myself with prayer, stretching, meditation, whatever it takes.

—*The X Change Rate*, **June 6, 2019**

[IN *BEWITCHED*, SAMANTHA IS] a really smart woman who is an ascendant master, dumbing down so she could fit in. She wanted a little dick. . . . And how many of us have lived *that* life, where we just wanted a little compassion, a little affection, and you dumbed yourself down?

—*What's the Tee?*, **March 20, 2019**

GOD IS THE word we use for that which cannot be described. So, it's *that thing*. And when you wanna fill that hole, pardon my French, there's only one thing that will fill it. And it ain't a 10-inch c—.

—*What's the Tee?*, **March 22, 2017**

YOU ARE NOT your thoughts and feelings. The true you is the awareness of them.

—**Twitter, February 22, 2019**

I'm in total awe of the human spirit's tenacity, and equally gobsmacked by the unrelenting audacity of the human ego.

—Twitter, October 15, 2015

HAVE YOU SEEN those nature documentaries where the lion finally gets the impala? There's a certain graceful surrender the prey takes on, like, "OK. There we are."

—**Buzzfeed News, June 2, 2015**

I'M NOT RELIGIOUS AT ALL, but that doesn't stop me from dropping to my knees & praying my black ass off.

—**Twitter, December 6, 2011**

STORY OF THE crucifixion is meaningless without the resurrection. I love a good comeback story.

—**Twitter, April 8, 2012**

THROUGH MUCH DESPAIR, I've learned that my best defense is to keep the playing field even, and maintain a balance by nurturing my higher Self. I get down on my knees and pray to disarm my Ego. When I physically kneel down to acknowledge a Higher Power, my Ego involuntarily submits.

—***GuRu*, October 23, 2018**

THERE'S A DIFFERENCE between knowing
the path and walking the path, and a bigger
difference between walking the path and sissying
that walk.

—**Twitter, May 11, 2016**

YESTERDAY DOESN'T EXIST—Tomorrow never
comes—There is only today—Now let these
bitches have it!

—**Twitter, October 30, 2011**

Media and Pop Culture

AND THE TRUTH is, Hollywood doesn't have
a moral responsibility, they have a monetary
responsibility. So they do things that make sense
to them financially.

—*Vulture*, August 12, 2016

A PUBLIC WEANED on fairytales won't question
the logic of a PR stunt, as long as the stunt
satisfies their insatiable thirst 4 distraction.

—Twitter, July 27, 2012

EVERYBODY, EVEN IF you work at McDonald's or
Walmart, you are in some form of show business.

—*Time*, June 12, 2017

I LEARNED EVERYTHING I know from
watching television.

—Twitter, September 13, 2015

I WAS ALWAYS pointing out that the emperor has
no clothes, and I was asking other people, "Are you
looking at this? The emperor has no clothes!" And
I couldn't find other people to corroborate what I
was seeing until I saw *Monty Python* on PBS.

—*Hollywood Reporter* video, March 21, 2018

WILD THEORY: To brilliantly emulate human behavior on camera, an actor gives up the ability to act human in real life.

—**Twitter, March 9, 2017**

IN THE DEPTHS of my despair, [Oprah] was a shining beacon to me, and today I have an Oprah shrine in my home. For a start, she has a quality that can't be learned or knocked off by another person. It's totally her own.

—*Lettin' It All Hang Out*, **June 6, 1996**

THE ONLY PERSON who interests me in pop culture right now is Judge Judy. That's it. Because of the realness—she has kept the story of mankind. . . . She remembers the rules of civility.

—**Vulture, March 23, 2016**

IT SEEMED I couldn't get press on my album [*Red Hot*] unless I was willing to play into the role that the mainstream press has assigned to gay people, which is as servants of straight ideals.

—**WikiNews, October 6, 2007**

IT USED TO be that the mainstream pop culture would get gay lingo 10 years later . . . but now, because of social media, it's accelerated that pace. So *Drag Race* is responsible for Katie Couric saying, "Oh, you slay, you slay," or on the news they talk about "Oh, she's throwing shade," you know?

—BUILD Series, May 12, 2016

WELL, THE TRUTH is, kids, this is a sitcom, this is a comedy. . . . If you want representation, you do it yourself. It starts on a personal level. If you want to change the world, change your mind. *Your* mind. Not anyone else's mind. *Your* mind.

—*Huffington Post*, January 14, 2012

Gender and Sexuality

At this moment? I'm everything and nothing at all. I'm black, I'm white, I'm male, female. To me, seeing all the facets of yourself is the next level of our evolution— understanding who we really are.

—*O, The Oprah Magazine*, January 16, 2018

THE REALITY IS that I am a man. The illusion is that I am a woman. But of the two, the illusion is truer.

—*Lettin' It All Hang Out*, **June 6, 1996**

AS BOYS, WE were taught to fit our emotions into this tiny little box, because that somehow makes other people feel more comfortable. But I never wanted to do that.

—*GuRu*, **October 23, 2018**

OUR CULTURE'S DISPROPORTIONATE obsession with masculine bravado creates the stigma attached to feminine boys.

—**Twitter, October 13, 2011**

THERE IS A definite prejudice towards men who use femininity as part of their palette; their emotional palette, their physical palette.

—**WikiNews, October 6, 2007**

I'VE DEFINITELY FOUND more prejudice in our
culture from being gay than from being black
or from being a drag queen. . . . I believe it is
linked to the death of the goddess in our culture,
goddess energy.

—*InnerVIEWS*, **March 17, 2011**

WE ARE A culture who is obsessed with
masculine behavior. For a man to dress in what's
considered girls' clothes or whatever, that's
definitely looked down upon. But for a woman to
do it, it's completely different. . . . And the truth is
we're all doing it, but we have a judgment against
what's considered feminine or weak.

—**NPR, February 2, 2012**

ESPECIALLY IN OUR culture, women have been
trained and domesticated to believe that they
are second-class citizens. They are not; they are
equal parts of what makes this world work.

—*Grazia*, **June 1, 2015**

LGBTQ Culture

IT'S WHY JUDY Garland and Joan Crawford speak to us so much. There's a certain desperate, dark, painful element to these people that we can relate to. And in spite of that, they have overcome it and become glamorous, joyous, beautiful fun-loving people.

—*Daily Beast*, April 11, 2016

WE HAVE ALL been so desensitized by these kinds of tragedies, but the Pulse tragedy did hit me the hardest because they are my children and because they're all of our children. They are the children who have dared to dance to the beat of a different drummer.

—*Los Angeles Times*, August 10, 2016

THEY TALK SO much about acceptance now today and it's like, yes, but trust me—I'm old. It's superficial.

—*New York Times*, May 15, 2016

BIGGEST THREAT AGAINST gay people isn't what others do to us, the biggest threat is the self loathing & shame we inflict upon ourselves.

—Twitter, November 6, 2011

GAY PEOPLE WILL accept a straight pop star over a gay pop star, or they will accept a straight version of a gay thing, because there's still so much self-loathing.

—**Vulture, March 23, 2016**

BUT THE TRUTH is, the opposite of shame isn't pride. The opposite of shame is love. What we are doing is calling attention to love, that's the key to the Pride celebration.

—*The View*, **June 6, 2019**

WE'VE HAD THIS adolescent outlook on life for far too long and it's time for us to take the human race to the next level. I believe that LGBT people can do that.

—*Toronto Sun*, **July 2, 2016**

THROUGH THE SHOW, we get to reach a lot of kids just with the message of learning your history and knowing how to move forward by knowing what your history is, because the future belongs to those who can remember the past.

—*Interview*, **September 2, 2013**

WE ENCRYPT *DRAG Race* with the secret
language that kept gay people linked for many
years before the '80s. Gay people had to be
secretive. There was a certain way, a certain
vernacular, a certain approach to pop culture
that we maintained. We lost that in recent
years, but we encrypt our shows with that secret
language of our gay brothers and sisters past.

—Daily Beast, April 11, 2016

WE HAVE SOMETHING that they don't have. . . .
Our secret weapon is love, music, laughter,
joy. We have colors, we have dancing, we have
creativity, we have our imaginations. And those
things—don't discredit them—those are strong,
huge, powerful, moving forces. That's how we
inspire. We have spirit. That's what we have to
change this world.

—BUILD Series, June 6, 2019

We transcend labels, descriptions & limitations. We are everything and nothing at all.

—Twitter, July 15, 2018

[IN REFERENCE TO his decision to eliminate the use of the term "she-mail" from *Drag Race*, an entendre formerly used on the show for messages that arrived for contestants] If you need me to change a word, I'll do it, if that makes you feel better. Life is too short.

—Buzzfeed News, June 2, 2015

[ON LANCE BASS using the word "tranny"] Words—it goes back to grade school: Sticks and stones, you know the rest. . . . And unfortunately in our culture one person can write a letter to the network and they shut something down. It's unfortunate. But I love the word "tranny."

—*Huffington Post*, January 14, 2012

AND IN THE ACT UP age we called ourselves queers because we earned the right, we took the word back. But in reality, once you go even deeper, you know, you have to come from intent. . . . But if you're offended by someone calling you a "tranny," it was only because you believe you are a "tranny!" So then, the solution is: Change your mind about yourself being a "tranny."

—*Huffington Post*, January 14, 2012

EACH MORNING I pray to set aside everything I THINK I know, so I may have an open mind and a new experience. I understand and regret the hurt I have caused. The trans community are heroes of our shared LGBTQ movement. You are my teachers.

—Twitter, March 5, 2018

IT WAS OBVIOUS that we, as a culture, have a hard time trying to understand the difference between a drag queen, transsexual, and a transgender, yet we find it very easy to know the difference between the American baseball league and the National baseball league, when they are both so similar.

—WikiNews, October 6, 2007

WE AS GAY people, we get to choose our family, you know, we get to choose the people that we're around, you know what I'm saying? I am your family. We are family here.

—RuPaul's Drag Race, March 11, 2013

IF [THE GAY CLUBS] were savable you bitches would've been paying money to go there and they would have made money and it would have worked.

—Buzzfeed News, June 2, 2015

THERE'S NOT ENOUGH dancing in the world. And the fact that there are no daytime discos right now is indicative of the trouble we're in as a society.

—*GuRu*, October 23, 2018

Politics

I'm making a political statement, everytime I make my booty pop.

—Twitter, February 24, 2012

WE'RE ALL BORN equal, then 15 minutes later, things change.

—**Twitter, January 18, 2016**

CAN WE PLEASE have an evolved discussion about what's really happening to our world? #CollectiveConsciousnessShift

—**Twitter, July 15, 2016**

IF YOU'VE EVER seen what the political process is, it is the most boring, horrible thing. And, it's . . . about compromising your own personal integrity. And listen, I do enough of that in Hollywood.

—***Marie Claire*, March 14, 2017**

REAL POLITICS IS what happens in the hearts and minds of people. Government politics is actually just power brokering and leverage peddling.

—**Twitter, July 7, 2016**

I learned years ago, I can't change the world. I can change my mind, but **I ain't concerned with other people.**

—*The Daily Show with Trevor Noah*, March 22, 2018

Actions speak louder than tweets.

—*The View*, June 6, 2019

DRAGSOLUTELY WORK THAT voting booth, but
just know that real political power is expressed
at the cash register. #SupportYourLocalFreaks

—**Twitter, October 26, 2015**

I DROPPED OUT of society when Reagan got in
office, and I've been underground ever since.

—*Geraldo*, **April 17, 1990**

WELL, YOU KNOW, during the '80s, it was
colorless, you know, with the Reagan regime
and all that stuff. And now people are busting
out. The pendulum swung so far to the right, it's
gonna come crashing back to the left, OK?

—*The Arsenio Hall Show*, **May 28, 1993**

WE ALL PLAYED a part in the Bush fiasco.
We can't just point the finger at what they did;
we have to take responsibility for our part.

—*Curve*, **January 20, 2009**

Political policies are like hemlines and hairstyles: They change with the trends. So it's hard to take any of it seriously.

—*Huffington Post,* January 14, 2012

I WASN'T READY to do a reality show during the
mean-spirited times of the Bush era. Especially
since during the fear-saturated era, gender
exploration usually had to go underground.
I knew I needed to stay away from that.

—*TV Guide*, February 1, 2010

I THOUGHT IT was time after these eight years
with the Bush administration, these eight years of
fear, that a new generation be introduced to drag.

—*Curve*, January 20, 2009

IT'S A REALLY weird time to be alive. For
someone like Obama to survive—he's a very
smart man—he's had to do some dumb things
because people, people don't want the truth.
It's the same thing with drag.

—*Huffington Post*, January 14, 2012

WHAT I DIDN'T count on was that post-9/11, there was this sort of hostile fear identity that this country especially took on. And it took many years for that to sort of wind down for this show [*RuPaul's Drag Race*] to happen. And, listen, I've been around for a long time, the pendulum always swings. Will it swing back to that type of small, closed window? More than likely it will.

—*New York Times* **video, May 6, 2013**

THE BEST POLITICAL minds in this country are rarely voted into office simply because they have sex and drugs in their background.

—**Twitter, December 19, 2014**

AND IF YOU think that you can go to fucking Washington and be rainbows and butterflies the whole time, you're living in a fucking fantasy world.... So, what do I think of Hillary? I think she's fucking awesome. Is she in bed with Wall Street? Goddammit, I should hope so!

—**Vulture, August 12, 2016**

My lips are overdrawn to distract from my obvious disdain for the Electoral College.

—Twitter, December 6, 2016

EVEN IF [TRUMP] wins, it will only accelerate the forward movement they're trying to defend against. What you resist persists.

—Twitter, November 7, 2016

IT'S ALL THROUGHOUT the whole Trump thing: Ego wants to divide us up. Ego wants to believe that we're separate from one another, but the truth is there's only one of us here.

—Vulture, August 12, 2016

WE LIVE IN an egocentric culture, and Trump is the poster boy of that egocentric culture.

—*Marie Claire*, March 14, 2017

AS A KID, I couldn't understand how the world could stand by and allow a Hitler to happen. Now I do.

—Twitter, November 11, 2016

FAIRYTALES, BOOKS, TV & religion, taught us all to know what a "bad guy" looks like, yet we overrode that basic training & put a villain in the White House anyway. WTF? There is a fatal flaw in our collective ability to judge character.

—**Twitter, January 2, 2018**

THE GREAT DIVIDE is between those who accept the now, and those who are being dragged, kicking and screaming into the 21st-century.

—**Twitter, July 17, 2016**

[ON THE 2016 PRESIDENTIAL ELECTION] It's as if they voted to bring back the horse & buggy to avoid learning to drive a car.

—**Twitter, December 1, 2016**

I *DO KNOW* that humans feel more comfortable in fear than they do in love. They feel more comfortable in their smallness than they do in their greatness, and that's very sad but it's just a fact.

—***Dazed*, June 1, 2015**

I THINK THE people who voted for Trump are the people who are not willing to move forward into this evolutionary period of our lives on this planet.

—*Marie Claire*, **March 14, 2017**

THE 20TH CENTURY energetically ended on 9/11/01, but this presidential election represents its last gasp.

—**Twitter, November 3, 2016**

A LOT OF the kids grew up in an age of Obama: they didn't know any better. So I guess this is what had to happen. There will be a lot of blood before we turn this around, unfortunately.

—*Vanity Fair*, **March 13, 2017**

Why is it that people who've been oppressed take on the same characteristics as their oppressors?

—Twitter, June 7, 2015

WHEN IT GETS down to survival, you have to pick your battles, and you don't pick battles with your allies. And I think, as the Trump era moves on, your allies and your enemies will become more and more evident.

—*Time*, **June 12, 2017**

THERE'S SO MUCH divisiveness in the world right now. I wanna be part of the mending of that.

—**ET Online, May 27, 2019**

AS SOON AS the lights go out, you'll see how advanced people's thinking is. This so-called "*Will & Grace* acceptance" era is just people fucking posing.

—**Vulture, March 23, 2016**

PEOPLE WILL HAVE you think, "Oh, we're fashion. We're gay. That's my gay over there!" It's like, no. We're still a very, very, very primitive culture.

—**Vulture, March 23, 2016**

MY THING IS, I think that this whole administration will actually accelerate what they're trying to defend against. What you defend against persists, and I think it's a call to action for all of the like-minded people like ourselves to get involved. Ultimately—and I've gotta think this way—it's probably the best thing that could have happened, because it shapes us up.

—*Vanity Fair*, **March 13, 2017**

OUR CRIMINAL JUSTICE system is a joke that's not at all funny.

—**Twitter, June 17, 2017**

HOW DARE SOME man tell a woman what to do with her body. That is outrageous! Outrageous.

—*Marie Claire*, **March 14, 2017**

PLANNED PARENTHOOD REPRESENTED so much freedom for us. For me to watch [my mother] blossom into a working woman and self-sufficient after this sort of system of being married to a man and staying home, after that façade fell apart, she built herself back up.

—*Marie Claire*, **March 14, 2017**

Secrets of Success

I knew that I wanted **love to be my platform.**

—BUILD Series, May 12, 2016

THERE IS A shield of protection that
has always been around me.

—**Buzzfeed News, June 2, 2015**

WELL, THE FIRST thing I would say to a young
person who is trying to find the rhythm, hit their
mark—what you need to do is to know thyself.
Know your rhythm. Know what it is that makes
you, you. Also, don't become bitter, because
you have every right to become bitter, and your
mind will tell you, "F this, f all of this." Don't
take the bait.

—*It Got Better*, **June 3, 2015**

I DON'T REALLY care about [the younger
generation]. The truth is, they're on their own.
They'll figure it out.

—**Vulture, March 23, 2016**

I TRY TO keep one step ahead of my internal
saboteur with prayer meditation yoga gym sleep
water & healthy food.

—**Twitter, April 5, 2012**

I LIKE THE solitude of the morning. It's quiet, I get to meditate. I see my trainer at 5 o'clock in the morning and we have the whole gym to ourselves, and I get to play all my music, and we are kiki-ing. I taught him how to cha-cha last week.

—*The X Change Rate*, **June 6, 2019**

THE FIRST THING I do in the morning is to stretch. Get everything opened up. It's important because if you don't feel good, usually it's because there's some blockage and you have to physically open up that blockage. Once your frequency is open, then the love will flow through you.

—*Grazia*, **June 1, 2015**

BEING YOUTHFUL HAS everything to do w/being flexible, both literally & figuratively. I've met plenty of "young people" who are old farts.

—**Twitter, November 7, 2011**

I wish every Starbucks location also had an adjacent disco—U could pop in for 15 minutes & just work it out.

—Twitter, December 20, 2011

Keep an open mind, you never know where that next big idea is coming from.

—Twitter, December 27, 2013

THERE'S A CERTAIN detachment sensitive
people must maintain to endure the harsh reality
of this f%ked up world.

—Twitter, April 10, 2015

ONE HELPFUL TECHNIQUE I use is to look at old
pictures of myself and remember the "conflama"
(conflict and drama) that was going on when the
photo was taken. In hindsight, those issues seem
small and inconsequential.

—*Workin' It! RuPaul's Guide to Life, Liberty,
and the Pursuit of Style*, February 2, 2019

I SAY, "LISTEN. Find out what it is you have that
makes you unique and special, and cultivate
that. And bring that out and then bring that to
the party."

—*The Oprah Winfrey Show*, 1995

WHAT MOST PEOPLE are doing is they're
playing small. They're playing a small version of
themselves for whatever reason. Whatever floats
your boat, you can do that if you want. But if you
want a show, you better tell somebody!

—BUILD Series, June 6, 2019

FOR YEARS, I sat around waiting for someone to discover me—WRONG. I discovered myself. Just like Dorothy in *The Wizard of Oz*, she went through all this time to find out that she had the power within her all along.

—*Tracking*, 1985

WHEN I WAS down, I was simply, from my point of view, a superstar in exile. When the rest of the world didn't know I was a star, I conducted myself as one, believing that sooner or later the rest of the world would catch up with me.

—*Lettin' It All Hang Out*, June 6, 1996

WHY COULDN'T I become a mainstream pop star in drag? Who said it couldn't be done? Was it all my own limited thinking that prevented me from moving forward? The answer was a resounding *yes*.

—*Workin' It! RuPaul's Guide to Life, Liberty, and the Pursuit of Style*, February 2, 2019

I do my own things. I create my own stuff. So I never counted on the industry or the status quo to say, you know, "We want you, play with us." I've always played with myself.

—NowThis News, October 25, 2018

I CLIMBED UP onstage for money 36 years ago and I've been doing it ever since.

—**NowThis News, October 25, 2018**

I LEARNED EARLY on that if I was embarassed by something, it was definitely something I needed to do. I needed to challenge myself in every single way I possibly could and take it as far as I possibly could.

—*GuRu*, **October 23, 2018**

LISTEN, I'M NOT the greatest actor. I'm not the greatest singer. I'm not the greatest drag queen. I'm not the greatest dancer. My gift has been having the clarity to hear the universe's stage directions and to take advantage of that.

—*Guardian*, **March 3, 2018**

Amazing talent & a great work ethic really helps, but I believe it mostly takes luck, which explains why most top dogs are so insecure.

—Twitter, April 17, 2012

YOU KNOW, THE truth is people vote for their friends. When I was in ninth grade, I won best afro and best dancer and I know I had both, but that's not what won me the award. What won me the award was I was hanging out with a cool crowd of kids. Don't get it twisted, that hasn't changed since junior high school.

—*Los Angeles Times*, August 10, 2016

YOU KNOW, BECAUSE it's been so long, I think I have an even deeper gratitude and understanding of how difficult and lucky it is to hit gold twice in one lifetime.

—*Interview*, September 2, 2013

MY BIGGEST CHALLENGE is staying interested in all this.

—*New York Times*, August 5, 2011

I THINK THAT'S why I've been able to stick around for so long, because I do music, I write, I produce, and I'm able to host. And, you know, it's important for young people to understand, to develop lots of different skills, and know thyself. Know the different areas of your consciousness that you can sell to people. You know, like prostitution.

—BUILD Series, May 12, 2016

YOU'VE GOT TO set yourself up so that you can do a lot of different things. Think Jane Fonda, think Quincy Jones, who has done everything. The old thing was that you would choose one thing to do for your life and you would do that forever. But life isn't that way anymore.

—BUILD Series, May 12, 2016

I like to keep moving, keep working, because it keeps the voices at bay. **You have to outrun the voices, the saboteur.**

—*Watch What Happens Live with Andy Cohen,*
March 7, 2017

YOU NEVER KNOW where that next big idea is coming from. So, I went and auditioned for stuff for this current pilot season. Who knows what will come of it.

—*Vanity Fair*, March 13, 2017

YOU DO A lot of projects. Most projects do not work, which is fine. Some do, some don't. You just go in and you do your best and you see what happens. If it works, great. If it doesn't, that's OK! But I'm having a great time.

—ET Online, May 27, 2019

SACRIFICES HAVE TO be made if you want to make a dent in the world, and that's what I started out to do—to make a dent in pop culture. I've done hanging out, I've done slacking—I love to work.

—*Independent*, August 1, 2015

HOLIDAYS ARE FOR people who actually have jobs! I never really had one of those.

—Vice, October 16, 2016

IF THEY OFFER me a job I'm gonna take it.

> —*Jimmy Kimmel Live*, December 3, 2018

I DON'T TURN down jobs. I will work until I can't work no more.

> —*Watch What Happens Live with Andy Cohen*,
> March 7, 2017

WHENEVER I'VE BEEN in charge of a team or employees, I keep the boundaries firmly in place while maintaining a comfortable, nonstressed atmosphere. I don't do tension and stress.

> —*Workin' It! RuPaul's Guide to Life, Liberty,
> and the Pursuit of Style*, February 2, 2019

I WAS SELFISHLY addicted to the adrenaline rush and the thrill of trying to beat the clock. Once I blew the lid off myself, I started enforcing a no-tardiness rule. I'd leave for appointments early, even if it meant I'd have to arrive early and wait in the parking lot.

> —*Workin' It! RuPaul's Guide to Life, Liberty,
> and the Pursuit of Style*, February 2, 2019

Every time you see me out socializing, I'm faking it, because I'm an introvert masquerading as an extrovert. So it takes a lot of battery power to do it.

—*Watch What Happens Live with Andy Cohen*, May 13, 2019

I like to arrive 10 minutes early just to let bitches know **who the f%k they dealin' wit**.

—Twitter, September 13, 2016

I HAVE NO problem saying, for the past 25 years,
I've been the number one b in the game. Number
one, still.

—**Television Academy Foundation, June 3, 2019**

FLEXIBILITY IS YOUR best defense against financial
ruin.

—**Twitter, October 24, 2015**

I GREW UP hearing all the stories of the Motown
stars who had squandered their fortunes and
were left penniless and I was dead set on not
becoming another show business statistic by
following in their footsteps.

—*Workin' It! RuPaul's Guide to Life, Liberty,*
and the Pursuit of Style, **February 2, 2019**

HAVING MONEY IS great when you have an
imagination.

—*New York Times*, **January 24, 2018**

CREATIVELY, I FOCUS on projects that get me excited and feed my desire for beauty, laughter, and love. Financially, I focus on intellectual properties that will bring revenue without me having to physically be there to collect the cash.

> —*Workin' It! RuPaul's Guide to Life, Liberty, and the Pursuit of Style*, February 2, 2019

THE TRUTH IS that success is something between you and your own butthole. Only you know how far you've come. Only you know how far you want to go. Only you know what lesson there is to be learned.

> —*Lettin' It All Hang Out*, June 6, 1996

TO GET THE acknowledgment from the establishment, it sort of feels kind of weird. Because it's not like all of a sudden I have to really care and focus on what they think of me, 'cause I've created my career without them—the establishment—giving me validation.

> —*Billboard* Facebook Live, August 16, 2016

The fame, the money, all the stuff: after a while—I've been doing this 34 years— **it's about the legacy work.**

—Daily Beast, April 11, 2016

Words of Wisdom

Kindness is first on my list of human virtues. A big fat ass is a close second.

—Twitter, June 16, 2015

Is THE GLASS half full or half empty? Both choices are correct, but one choice will bring you joy, and the other will bring you pain. Yep, I choose joy.

—*Workin' It! RuPaul's Guide to Life, Liberty, and the Pursuit of Style*, February 2, 2019

ONE BY ONE I had to recalibrate my belief system, and that is why most people won't do it, because it is really difficult. Because you really get to know who you are, what you're made of, where your limitations are. And who wants to do that? Usually, no one wants to do that. But I tell you, that is the key to expanding your experience in this life.

—LA Made, June 25, 2017

BIGGEST CHALLENGE AFTER discovering IT IS ALL AN ILLUSION is to constantly summon the joy & to not let anger & bitterness engulf U.

—Twitter, July 16, 2012

If someone says you're beautiful, believe them. If someone says you're ugly, don't believe them.

—Twitter, October 16, 2016

Being vulnerable is power.

—NowThis News, October 25, 2018

BEING "OVERLY SENSITIVE" was a blessing & a curse until I learned: I am not my feelings—I am actually the awareness of my feelings.

—Twitter, February 26, 2012

WE'RE ALL BORN with a GPS system, and it's your job to learn how to navigate with it.

—BUILD Series, May 12, 2016

BEING 54, AT some point you learn to trust the first thing that comes into your head.

—*Independent*, August 1, 2015

THE BIGGEST OBSTACLES I have ever faced were the ones placed there by me.

—BUILD Series, June 6, 2019

WHEN THE UNIVERSE speaks to you, don't second-guess and go, "That'll never work. That'll *never* work." Listen. Listen to it and put it into motion.

—BUILD Series, June 6, 2019

THE PEOPLE WHO are able to die a thousand deaths and become reborn a thousand times are the real shot callers in this life.

—**LA Made, June 25, 2017**

YOU HAVE TO be willing to unload some of the things that don't work anymore. Like a rocket gets propelled into space with the fuselage, but once it gets to a certain place in the journey, the fuselage has to break off so that it can move forward. You can't keep the fuselage, doll!

—**NowThis News, October 25, 2018**

LISTEN, LIFE IS hard, and life is hard whether you choose to be a shot caller or to sit at home and watch daytime television all day; it's hard.

—*Marketplace*, **October 23, 2018**

KNOWING WHAT YOU want to do in life is usually not difficult. What is difficult is carving out the time it takes to invest in you.

—*Grazia*, **June 1, 2015**

Number one: Pay your taxes. Number two: **Don't read the comments.**

—BUILD Series, June 6, 2019

I DON'T THINK my destiny has really happened yet. But the most difficult choice I make every day is to be engaged, choose love, and not succumb to darkness. Because it's always in my peripheral vision.

—*O, The Oprah Magazine*, January 16, 2018

Milestones

1960

- RuPaul Andre Charles is born on November 17, 1960, in San Diego, California, to Ernestine "Toni" Charles and Irving Charles.

1967

- RuPaul's parents divorce, and he and his three sisters live with their mother in a tract home in San Diego.

1975

- RuPaul moves to Atlanta, Georgia, with his sister Renetta and attends the Northside School of Performing Arts.

1982

- RuPaul makes his TV debut on *The American Music Show*—a variety show on Atlanta public access TV—where he will make regular appearances over the following years. In Atlanta, he also regularly performs at the Celebrity Club, which is managed by friend and DJ Larry Tee.

1983

- During these years in Atlanta, RuPaul struggles as a filmmaker and a musician, performing sporadically with his band the U-Hauls, and then with the newly formed Wee Wee Pole.

1984

- RuPaul moves to New York but returns to Atlanta after six months. During this time, he begins to develop his original drag character, undercover model "Starrbooty."

1987

- RuPaul returns to New York and begins working as a go-go dancer.

- RuPaul creates the film trilogy *RuPaul Is: Starrbooty!*, which stars RuPaul, Lady Bunny, and Larry Tee.

- RuPaul appears at Wigstock, an outdoor drag festival hosted by his former Atlanta roommate, Lady Bunny, in the East Village of New York City. RuPaul will continue to make appearances at this festival over the next several years.

1988

- RuPaul moves to Los Angeles and performs on *The Gong Show*. He briefly lives in San Diego before moving back to New York at the encouragement of Larry Tee.

1989

- RuPaul is featured in the music video for "Love Shack" by the B-52s.

- RuPaul is crowned "Queen of Manhattan" by a group of New York–based club owners and promoters.

1990

- RuPaul appears with other members of the "Club Kids" on the *Geraldo* show.

1991

- Fenton Bailey and Randy Barbato, RuPaul's longtime friends and managers from Atlanta, create the production company World of Wonder.

- RuPaul signs a recording contract with Tommy Boy Records.

1992

- RuPaul's first single, "Supermodel (You Better Work)," is released by Tommy Boy Records. The song becomes one of 1993's top-selling dance records and peaks at number 45 on the Billboard Hot 100.

1993

- RuPaul appears on *The Arsenio Hall Show*, a late-night talk show.

- RuPaul's first studio album, *Supermodel of the World*, is released.

- RuPaul performs "Supermodel (You Better Work)" at the March on Washington for Lesbian, Gay, and Bi Equal Rights and Liberation.

1994

- RuPaul becomes the face of MAC Cosmetics' Viva Glam line, becoming the first drag queen ever to become the face of a major cosmetic line.

- RuPaul meets future husband Georges LeBar on a dance floor at Limelight in New York City.

- RuPaul appears in Spike Lee's film *Crooklyn*.

1995

- RuPaul appears in several feature films, including *The Brady Bunch Movie*; *To Wong Foo, Thanks for Everything! Julie Newmar*; and *Blue in the Face*, and in the documentary *Wigstock: The Movie*.

1996

- RuPaul begins hosting a morning radio show on New York's WKTU with Michelle Visage.

- *Lettin' It All Hang Out*, RuPaul's first book, is published.

- RuPaul appears at the VH1 Fashion and Music Awards.

- *The RuPaul Show* launches with Michelle Visage, making RuPaul the first openly gay talk show host on national television. Guests on the show include Cher, Diana Ross, Bea Arthur, Dionne Warwick, the Backstreet Boys, and Nirvana.

- RuPaul's second studio album, *Foxy Lady*, is released by Rhino Records.

1997

- RuPaul releases a Christmas covers album, *Ho Ho Ho*.

1998

- *The RuPaul Show* is canceled due to difficulty making ad sales and booking guests.

1999

- RuPaul receives the Vito Russo Award at the GLAAD Media Awards for his work in promoting equality within the LGBTQ community.

- RuPaul appears in cult film *But I'm a Cheerleader*.

- RuPaul takes a hiatus to spend time with his family and reconnect with friends.

2004

- RuPaul releases album *Red Hot* via his label RuCo, Inc.—his first new release since the late '90s. Moving forward, he releases all new music from his own record label.

2005

- Logo TV, an LGBTQ-focused network, launches.

2006

- World of Wonder hires Tom Campbell as head of development; Campbell begins to discuss show ideas with RuPaul.

- RuPaul releases *RuPaul.ReWorked,* which features remixes of his back catalog hits plus new recordings.

2007

- RuPaul releases *Starrbooty,* the fourth movie in the *Starrbooty* series.

2009

- RuPaul launches *RuPaul's Drag Race*, which premieres on Logo TV.
- *Champion*, RuPaul's fifth studio album, is released, and it reaches number 12 on the Billboard Top Dance/Electronic Albums chart.

2010

- *Workin' It! RuPaul's Guide to Life, Liberty, and the Pursuit of Style* is published.
- *RuPaul's Drag U*, a spin-off of *RuPaul's Drag Race* that features women getting drag makeovers, premieres on Logo TV.

2011

- *Glamazon*, RuPaul's sixth studio album, is released.

2012

- *RuPaul's Drag Race All Stars*, a spin-off of *RuPaul's Drag Race* that invites past *Drag Race* contestants to compete, premieres on Logo TV.

2013

- RuPaul debuts GLAMAZON, a beauty collection and unisex fragrance, with ColorEvolution.

2014

- *Born Naked*, RuPaul's seventh studio album and best-charting album to date, is released.

- RuPaul receives accusations of transphobia after he uses the term "shemale" on *RuPaul's Drag Race*. Accusations also point to the show's continued use of the "You've got she-mail" phrase. RuPaul apologizes and Logo TV removes the phrase.

- RuPaul launches a podcast, *RuPaul: What's the Tee?*, with cohost Michelle Visage.

2015

- RuPaul's eighth studio album, *Realness*, is released, timed to coincide with the premiere of season seven of *RuPaul's Drag Race*. RuPaul will continue to time album releases with season premieres.

- RuPaul launches *Good Work*, a plastic surgery–themed talk show, on E!

- *Slay Belles*, RuPaul's second Christmas album, is released.

2016

- RuPaul's 10th studio album, *Butch Queen*, is released.

- *Gay for Play Game Show Starring RuPaul* launches on Logo TV.

- RuPaul wins an Emmy for *RuPaul's Drag Race* for Outstanding Host for a Reality or Reality-Competition Program.

2017

- *Drag Race* moves from Logo TV to VH1 for the ninth season, and the season premiere has one million viewers.

- RuPaul releases *Remember Me: Essential, Vol. 1,* a collection of new songs and remakes of previously released music. A few months later, he releases *Essential, Vol. 2.*

- RuPaul's album *American* is released, partly as a response to the 2016 US presidential election.

- RuPaul appears on the Netflix series *Girlboss* and serves alongside J. J. Abrams as executive producer of an autobiographical series about his rise to prominence in the 1980s club scene.

- RuPaul is among the honorees of the *Time* 100 list.

- RuPaul releases *Starrbooty: Original Motion Picture Soundtrack.*

- *Gay for Play* ends after two seasons.

2018

- RuPaul becomes the first drag star to be inducted into the Hollywood Walk of Fame.

- RuPaul comes under fire from the trans community after responding that he would "probably not" allow a trans woman who had begun the process of transitioning to compete on his show. He doubles down on this position, tweeting that the medical transitioning process is akin to taking "performance enhancing drugs," which would not be allowed "in the Olympics." He later apologizes and acknowledges he still has much to learn from the LGBTQ community.

- *RuPaul: What's the Tee?* wins a Webby Award for Best Host.

- RuPaul receives the Emmys for Outstanding Host for a Reality or Reality-Competition Program and Outstanding Reality-Competition Program for *RuPaul's Drag Race*.

- *GuRu*, RuPaul's third book, is published.

- RuPaul releases the album *Christmas Party*, which includes new music as well as remixes of previous Christmas tracks. A number of these songs are featured on *RuPaul's Drag Race Holi-slay Spectacular*, a holiday special on VH1.

2019

- A new RuPaul-hosted talk show, *RuPaul*, premieres on Fox on select stations.

Acknowledgments

We want to thank Kristina Dehlin and Emma Kupor
for their invaluable contributions to the preparation
of this manuscript.